INSTRUMENTAL

CD+ INSIDE

PLAY-ALONG

Top Hits fr
TV, Movies & Musicals
INSTRUMENTAL SOLOS

M000105832

Arranged by Bill Galliford and Ethan Neuburg
Recordings Produced by Dan Warner, Doug Emery and Lee Levin

© 2016 Alfred Music
All Rights Reserved. Printed in USA.

ISBN-10: 1-4706-3298-5
ISBN-13: 978-1-4706-3298-4

Alfred

Alfred Cares. Contents printed on environmentally responsible paper.

Contents

mp3 CD **Track**

ALL ABOUT THAT BASS

Track 2: Demo
Track 3: Play-Along

Words and Music by
MEGHAN TRAINOR and KEVIN KADISH

Moderately bright (♩ = 132)

6

AS TIME GOES BY

(from *Casablanca*)

Track 4: Demo
Track 5: Play-Along

Words and Music by
HERMAN HUPFELD

Slow ballad (♩ = 82)

Track 6: Demo
Track 7: Play-Along

ARTHUR'S THEME
(BEST THAT YOU CAN DO)

(from *Arthur*)

Words and Music by
BURT BACHARACH, CAROLE BAYER SAGER,
CHRISTOPHER CROSS and PETER ALLEN

Moderately slow, with a half-time feel (♩ = 68)

Arthur's Theme (Best That You Can Do) - 2 - 1

rit. e dim.

Track 8: Demo
Track 9: Play-Along

BLUEBERRY HILL

Words and Music by
AL LEWIS, VINCENT ROSE
and LARRY STOCK

Track 10: Demo
Track 11: Play-Along

BOTH SIDES, NOW

Words and Music by
JONI MITCHELL

poco rit.

Track 12: Demo
Track 13: Play-Along

BOULEVARD OF BROKEN DREAMS

Words by
BILLIE JOE

Music by
GREEN DAY

Moderately slow (♩ = 86)

19 *Chorus:*

Boulevard of Broken Dreams - 2 - 1

Track 14: Demo
Track 15: Play-Along

CAN YOU FEEL THE LOVE TONIGHT

(From Walt Disney's *The Lion King*)

Words by
TIM RICE

Music by
ELTON JOHN

CONCERNING HOBBITS

(from *The Lord of the Rings: The Fellowship of the Ring*)

Music by
HOWARD SHORE

Track 16: Demo
Track 17: Play-Along

CAN'T FIGHT THE MOONLIGHT

(from *Coyote Ugly*)

Words and Music by
DIANE WARREN

Track 18: Demo
Track 19: Play-Along

Can't Fight the Moonlight - 2 - 1

COOL KIDS

Track 20: Demo
Track 21: Play-Along

Words and Music by
GRAHAM SIEROTA, JAMIE SIEROTA,
NOAH SIEROTA, SYDNEY SIEROTA,
JEFFERY SIEROTA and JESIAH DZWONEK

Moderate rock (♩ = 126)

CORPSE BRIDE
(Main Title)

Music by
DANNY ELFMAN

Track 22: Demo
Track 23: Play-Along

DIAMONDS ARE FOREVER

Music by JOHN BARRY
Lyric by DON BLACK

FALLING SLOWLY

(from *Once*)

Track 26: Demo
Track 27: Play-Along

Words and Music by
GLEN HANSARD and
MARKÉTA IRGLOVÁ

DING-DONG! THE WITCH IS DEAD

(from *The Wizard of Oz*)

Track 28: Demo
Track 29: Play-Along

Music by HAROLD ARLEN
Lyric by E.Y. HARBURG

Moderately bright march (♩ = 116)

poco rit.

a tempo

Ding-Dong! The Witch Is Dead - 2 - 1

Track 30: Demo
Track 31: Play-Along

DON'T STOP BELIEVIN'

Words and Music by
JONATHAN CAIN, NEAL SCHON
and STEVE PERRY

Moderate rock (♩ = 120)

Don't Stop Believin' - 2 - 1

Don't Stop Believin' - 2 - 2

Track 32: Demo
Track 33: Play-Along

FAME
(from *Fame*)

Lyrics by
DEAN PITCHFORD

Music by
MICHAEL GORE

Moderate dance beat (♩ = 132)

FOLLOW THE YELLOW BRICK ROAD/ WE'RE OFF TO SEE THE WIZARD

(from *The Wizard of Oz*)

Music by HAROLD ARLEN
Lyric by E.Y. HARBURG

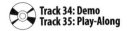

Track 34: Demo
Track 35: Play-Along

FOR YOUR EYES ONLY

Music by BILL CONTI
Lyrics by MICHAEL LEESON

GOLDFINGER

Music by JOHN BARRY
Lyrics by LESLIE BRICUSSE
and ANTHONY NEWLEY

GHOSTBUSTERS

Track 40: Demo
Track 41: Play-Along

Words and Music by
RAY PARKER, JR.

Who you gon - na call? Ghost - bust - ers!

Who you gon - na call? Ghost -

bust-ers!

Ghostbusters - 2 - 1

Track 42: Demo
Track 43: Play-Along

GONNA FLY NOW
(Theme from *Rocky*)

Words and Music by
BILL CONTI, AYN ROBBINS
and CAROL CONNORS

Moderately ♩ = 96

Gonna Fly Now - 2 - 1

THE GOOD, THE BAD AND THE UGLY

(Main Title)

Track 44: Demo
Track 45: Play-Along

By ENNIO MORRICONE

The Good, the Bad and the Ugly - 2 - 1

Track 46: Demo
Track 47: Play-Along

THE GREAT ESCAPE MARCH

(from *The Great Escape*)

Words by
AL STILLMAN

Music by
ELMER BERNSTEIN

Track 48: Demo
Track 49: Play-Along

THE GREATEST LOVE OF ALL

Words by
LINDA CREED

Music by
MICHAEL MASSER

Moderately slow (♩ = 64)

Track 50: Demo
Track 51: Play-Along

HE'S A PIRATE

(from Walt Disney Pictures' *Pirates of the Caribbean: The Curse of the Black Pearl*)

By KLAUS BADELT

Very bright (♩. = 138)

HEDWIG'S THEME
(from Harry Potter and the Sorcerer's Stone)

Music by
JOHN WILLIAMS

Track 52: Demo
Track 53: Play-Along

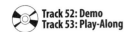

I DON'T WANT TO MISS A THING

(from Armageddon)

Words and Music by
DIANE WARREN

Track 54: Demo
Track 55: Play-Along

I Don't Want to Miss a Thing - 2 - 1

Track 56: Demo
Track 57: Play-Along

IN DREAMS
(from *The Lord of the Rings: The Fellowship of the Ring*)

Words and Music by
FRAN WALSH and
HOWARD SHORE

Moderately slow (♩ = 76)

*G♭ = F♯

JAMES BOND THEME

(from *Dr. No*)

By
MONTY NORMAN

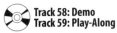

Track 60: Demo
Track 61: Play-Along

From Walt Disney's Frozen
LET IT GO

Music and Lyrics by
KRISTEN ANDERSON-LOPEZ
and ROBERT LOPEZ

Let It Go - 3 - 1

THE MAGNIFICENT SEVEN
(Main Title)

Track 62: Demo
Track 63: Play-Along

By ELMER BERNSTEIN

NOBODY DOES IT BETTER
(from *The Spy Who Loved Me*)

Track 64: Demo
Track 65: Play-Along

Music by MARVIN HAMLISCH
Lyrics by CAROLE BAYER SAGER

THE NOTEBOOK
(Main Title)

Written by
AARON ZIGMAN

Slowly, with expression (♩ = 69)

Track 68: Demo
Track 69: Play-Along

OVER THE RAINBOW

(from *The Wizard of Oz*)

Lyric by
E.Y. HARBURG

Music by
HAROLD ARLEN

Slowly, with expression ($\quarternote = 88$)

ROAR

Track 70: Demo
Track 71: Play-Along

Words and Music by
KATY PERRY, LUKASZ GOTTWALD,
MAX MARTIN, BONNIE McKEE
and HENRY WALTER

Moderate pop rock (♩ = 90)

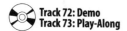
Track 72: Demo
Track 73: Play-Along

THE PRAYER

Words and Music by
CAROLE BAYER SAGER and DAVID FOSTER

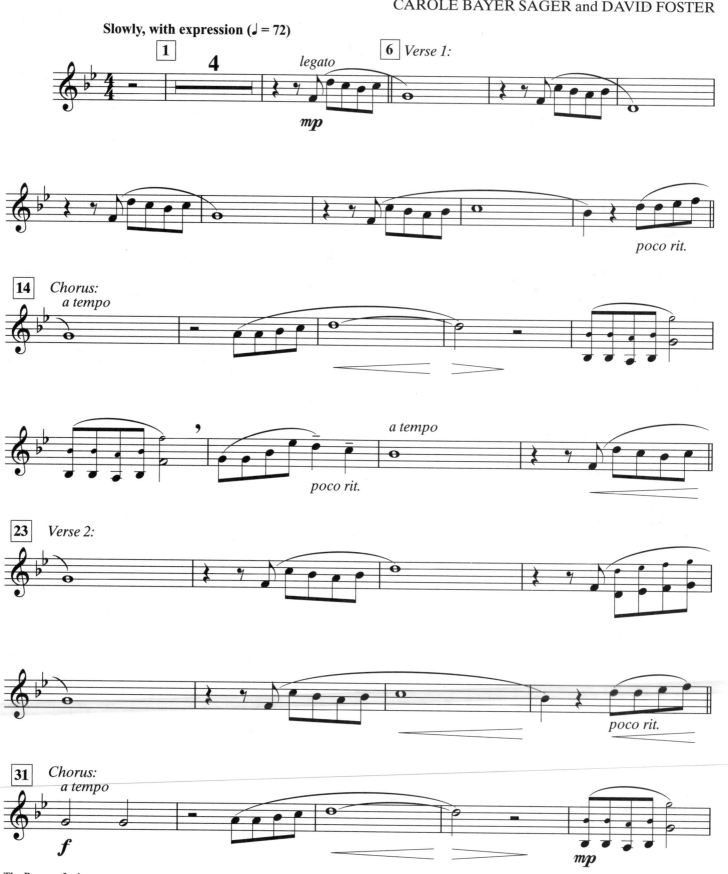

The Prayer - 2 - 1

(I CAN'T GET NO) SATISFACTION

Track 74: Demo
Track 75: Play-Along

Words and Music by
MICK JAGGER and KEITH RICHARDS

Moderately, driving (♩ = 132)

Track 76: Demo
Track 77: Play-Along

SONG FROM M*A*S*H
(Suicide Is Painless)

Words and Music by
MIKE ALTMAN and JOHNNY MANDEL

Track 78: Demo
Track 79: Play-Along

SEE YOU AGAIN
(from *Furious 7*)

Words and Music by
CAMERON THOMAZ, CHARLIE PUTH,
ANDREW CEDAR and JUSTIN FRANKS

See You Again - 2 - 1

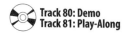

Track 80: Demo
Track 81: Play-Along

STAIRWAY TO HEAVEN

Words and Music by
JIMMY PAGE and ROBERT PLANT

Stairway to Heaven - 2 - 1

STAR WARS
(Main Theme)
(from *Star Wars Episode IV: A New Hope*)

Track 82: Demo
Track 83: Play-Along

Music by
JOHN WILLIAMS

Track 84: Demo
Track 85: Play-Along

SUMMERTIME
(from *Porgy and Bess*)

Music and Lyrics by
GEORGE GERSHWIN,
DuBOSE and DOROTHY HEYWARD
and IRA GERSHWIN

THEME FROM SUPERMAN

Music by
JOHN WILLIAMS

Theme from Superman - 2 - 1

Theme from Superman - 2 - 2

Track 88: Demo
Track 89: Play-Along

WE ARE YOUNG

Words and Music by
NATE RUESS, ANDREW DOST,
JACK ANTONOFF and JEFFREY BHASKER

We Are Young - 3 - 1

We Are Young - 3 - 2

66

We Are Young - 3 - 3

YOU ONLY LIVE TWICE

Music by JOHN BARRY
Lyric by LESLIE BRICUSSE

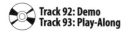
Track 92: Demo
Track 93: Play-Along

A WHITER SHADE OF PALE

Words and Music by
KEITH REID and GARY BROOKER

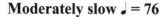

Moderately slow ♩ = 76

9 *Verse:*

A Whiter Shade of Pale - 2 - 1

A Whiter Shade of Pale - 2 - 2

THE WINDMILLS OF YOUR MIND
(from *The Thomas Crown Affair*)

Track 94: Demo
Track 95: Play-Along

Words by
ALAN and MARILYN BERGMAN

Music by
MICHEL LEGRAND

The Windmills of Your Mind - 2 - 1

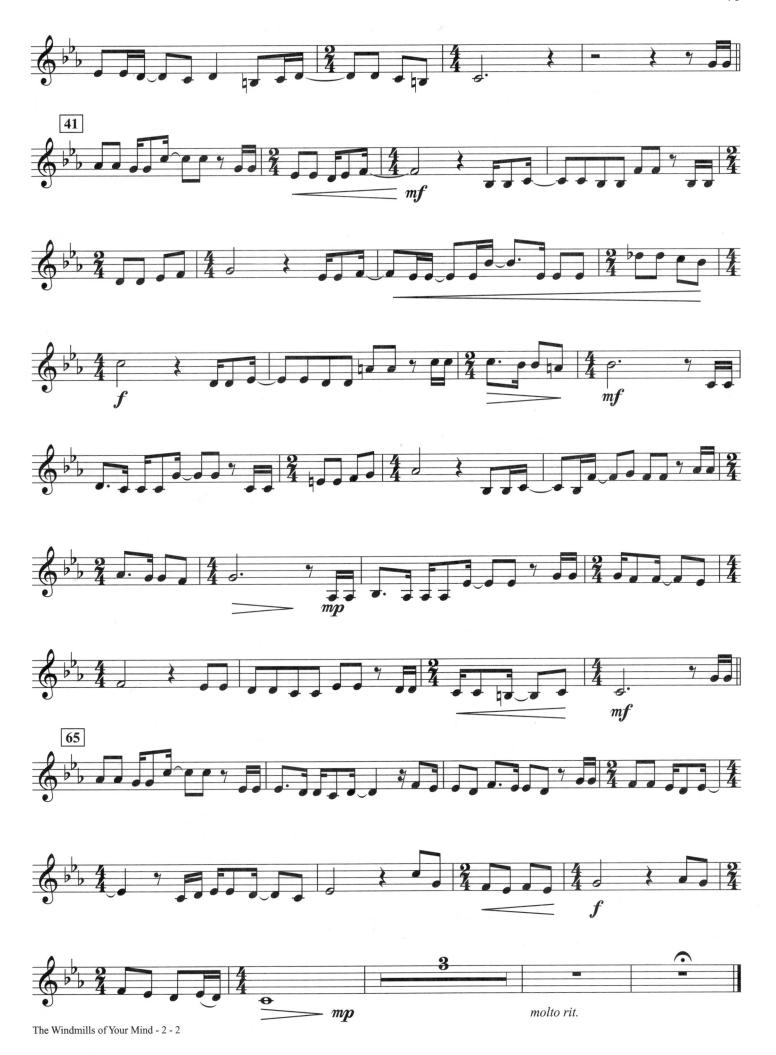

The Windmills of Your Mind - 2 - 2

YOU RAISE ME UP

Words and Music by
ROLF LOVLAND and
BRENDAN GRAHAM

YOU'VE GOT A FRIEND IN ME

(from Toy Story)

Words and Music by
RANDY NEWMAN

Track 98: Demo
Track 99: Play-Along

Easy shuffle (♩ = 108) (♫ = ♪♪)

PARTS OF THE HORN AND FINGERING CHART

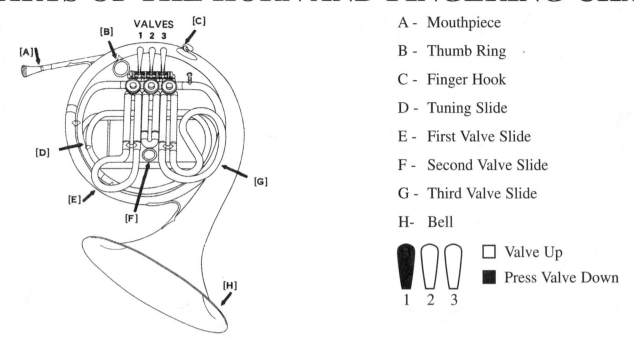

A - Mouthpiece

B - Thumb Ring

C - Finger Hook

D - Tuning Slide

E - First Valve Slide

F - Second Valve Slide

G - Third Valve Slide

H- Bell

☐ Valve Up

■ Press Valve Down

F Horns use the top fingerings. B♭ Horns use the bottom fingerings. F/B♭ Double Horns use the top fingerings without the thumb, or the bottom fingerings with the thumb. A good rule is to play notes from the second line G down on the F Horn, and from the second line G♯ up on the B♭ Horn.

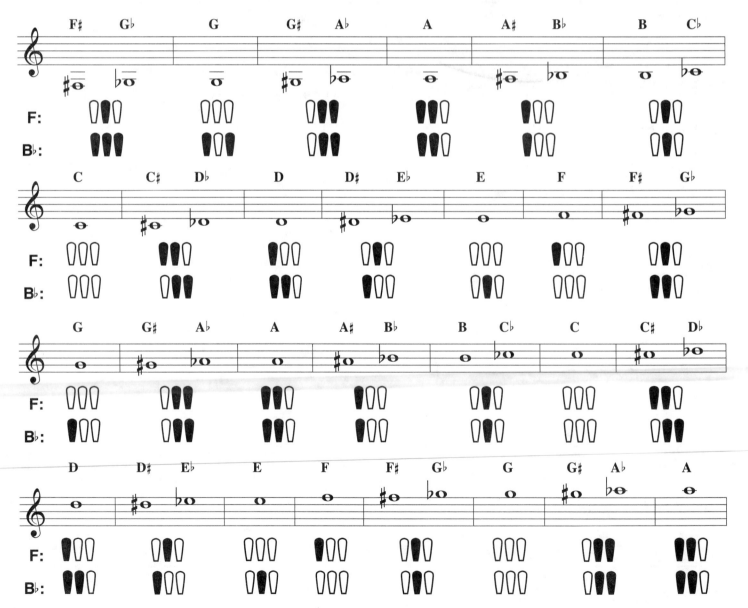

INSTRUMENTAL SOLOS

This instrumental series contains themes from Blizzard Entertainment's popular massively multiplayer online role-playing game and includes 4 pages of art from the World of Warcraft universe. The compatible arrangements are carefully edited for the Level 2–3 player, and include an accompaniment CD which features a demo track and play-along track. Titles: Lion's Pride • The Shaping of the World • Pig and Whistle • Slaughtered Lamb • Invincible • A Call to Arms • Gates of the Black Temple • Salty Sailor • Wrath of the Lich King • Garden of Life.

(00-36626) | Flute Book & CD | $12.99

(00-36629) | Clarinet Book & CD | $12.99

(00-36632) | Alto Sax Book & CD | $12.99

(00-36635) | Tenor Sax Book & CD | $12.99

(00-36638) | Trumpet Book & CD | $12.99

(00-36641) | Horn in F Book & CD | $12.99

(00-36644) | Trombone Book & CD | $12.99

(00-36647) | Piano Acc. Book & CD | $14.99

(00-36650) | Violin Book & CD | $16.99

(00-36653) | Viola Book & CD | $16.99

(00-36656) | Cello Book & CD | $16.99

Wrath of the Lich King, The Burning Crusade, World of Warcraft, and Blizzard Entertainment are trademarks and/or registered trademarks of Blizzard Entertainment, Inc., in the U.S. and/or other countries.

Harry Potter
INSTRUMENTAL SOLOS

Play-along with the best-known themes from the Harry Potter film series! The compatible arrangements are carefully edited for the Level 2–3 player, and include an accompaniment CD which features a demo track and play-along track.

Titles: Double Trouble • Family Portrait • Farewell to Dobby • Fawkes the Phoenix • Fireworks • Harry in Winter • Harry's Wondrous World • Hedwig's Theme • Hogwarts' Hymn • Hogwarts' March • Leaving Hogwarts • Lily's Theme • Obliviate • Statues • A Window to the Past • Wizard Wheezes.

(00-39211) | Flute Book & CD | $12.99
(00-39214) | Clarinet Book & CD | $12.99
(00-39217) | Alto Sax Book & CD | $12.99
(00-39220) | Tenor Sax Book & CD | $12.99
(00-39223) | Trumpet Book & CD | $12.99
(00-39226) | Horn in F Book & CD | $12.99
(00-39229) | Trombone Book & CD | $12.99
(00-39232) | Piano Acc. Book & CD | $18.99
(00-39235) | Violin Book & CD | $18.99
(00-39238) | Viola Book & CD | $18.99
(00-39241) | Cello Book & CD | $18.99